My
Peter Rabbit
Birthday Book

My
Peter Rabbit
Birthday Book

With new reproductions from the
original illustrations by
BEATRIX POTTER™

FREDERICK WARNE

FREDERICK WARNE

Penguin Books Ltd, Harmondsworth, Middlesex, England
Viking Penguin Inc., 40 West 23rd Street, New York, New York 10010, U.S.A.
Penguin Books Australia Ltd, Ringwood, Victoria, Australia
Penguin Books Canada Limited, 2801 John Street, Markham, Ontario, Canada L3R 1B4
Penguin Books (N.Z.) Ltd, 182–190 Wairau Road, Auckland 10, New Zealand

First published as *The Beatrix Potter Birthday Book*, 1974
Fifteenth reprint 1986
This edition with new reproductions first published 1987

LIBRARY OF CONGRESS CATALOG CARD NO. 73-89833

ISBN 0 7232 3523 6

Printed and bound in Great Britain by
William Clowes Ltd, Beccles and London

INTRODUCTION

All seasons of the year are pictured in
Beatrix Potter's books. Johnny Town-
mouse comes to visit Timmy Willie on a fine
spring day. Tom Kitten and his two little
sisters play in a summer garden where
pansies, forget-me-nots and carnations
bloom. Squirrel Nutkin and his friends
gather their harvest in the autumn woods,
and the Tailor of Gloucester walks through
streets where the sun is shining on the snow.

The pictures chosen for this little book
have been arranged in such a way that
those who write their names in it will be
reminded by the illustrations not only of the
season, but also of the month in which they
were born.

JANUARY

January 1

January 2

January 3

January 4

January 5

January 6

January 7

January 8

January 9

January 10

January 11

January 12

January 13

January 14

January 15

January 16

January 17

January 18

_____

_____

_____

January 19

_____

_____

_____

January 20

_____

_____

_____

January 21

_____

_____

_____

January 22

January 23

January 24

January 25

January 26

January 27

January 28

January 29

January 30

January 31

FEBRUARY

February 1

_____

_____

_____

February 2

_____

_____

_____

February 3

_____

_____

_____

February 4

February 5

February 6

February 7

February 8

_____

_____

_____

February 9

_____

_____

_____

February 10

_____

_____

_____

February 11

_____

_____

_____

February 12

February 13

February 14

February 15

February 16

February 17

"Then I will sing," replied Pig-wig.
"You will not mind if I say iddy
tidditty? I have forgotten some of
the words."

February 18

February 19

February 20

February 21

Pussy-cat sits by the fire

February 22

February 23

February 24

February 25

February 26

February 27

February 28

February 29

MARCH

March 1

March 2

March 3

March 4

March 5

March 6

March 7

March 8

March 9

March 10

March 11

March 12

March 13

March 14

March 15

March 16

March 17

March 18

March 19

March 20

_____

_____

_____

March 21

_____

_____

_____

March 22

March 23

March 24

March 25

March 26

March 27

March 28

March 29

March 30

March 31

The rain trickled down his
back, and for nearly an
hour he stared at the float.

APRIL

April 1

April 2

April 3

April 4

April 5

April 6

April 7

April 8

April 9

April 10

April 11

April 12

April 13

April 14

April 15

April 16

April 17

April 18

April 19

April 20

_____

_____

_____

April 21

_____

_____

_____

April 22

April 23

April 24

April 25

We have a little garden,
    A garden of our own
And every day we water there
    The seeds that we have sown.

April 26

April 27

April 28

April 29

The eight little pigs had
very fine appetites.

MAY

May 1

May 2

May 3

May 4

_____

_____

_____

May 5

_____

_____

_____

May 6

_____

_____

_____

May 7

_____

_____

_____

May 8

May 9

May 10

May 11

"When the sun comes out
again, you should see my
garden and the flowers –
roses and pinks and pansies."

May 12

_____

_____

May 13

_____

_____

May 14

_____

_____

May 15

_____

_____

May 16

May 17

May 18

May 19

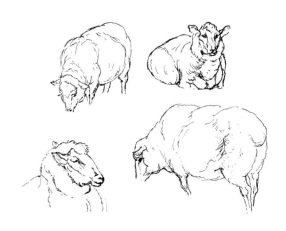

May 20

_____

_____

_____

May 21

_____

_____

_____

May 22

May 23

May 24

May 25

Mr McGregor hung up
the little jacket and the
shoes for a scare-crow to
frighten the blackbirds.

May 26

May 27

May 28

May 29

May 30

_____

_____

_____

May 31

_____

_____

_____

JUNE

June 1

_____

_____

_____

June 2

_____

_____

_____

June 3

_____

_____

_____

June 4

June 5

June 6

June 7

June 8

June 9

June 10

June 11

June 12

June 13

June 14

June 15

June 17

June 18

June 19

June 20

June 21

June 22

June 23

June 24

June 25

June 26

June 27

June 28

June 29

_____

_____

_____

June 30

_____

_____

_____

JULY

July 1

July 2

July 3

July 4

July 5

July 6

July 7

July 8

July 9

July 10

July 11

July 12

_____

_____

July 13

_____

_____

July 14

_____

_____

July 15

_____

_____

_____

July 16

_____

_____

_____

July 17

_____

_____

_____

July 18

July 19

July 20

July 21

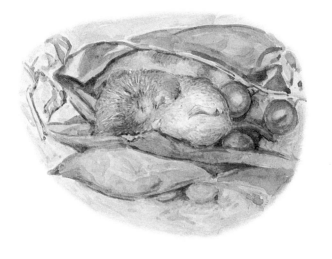

After eating some peas
– Timmy Willie fell
fast asleep.

July 22

July 23

July 24

July 25

July 26

_____

_____

_____

July 27

_____

_____

_____

July 28

_____

_____

_____

July 29

_____

_____

_____

July 30

July 31

AUGUST

August 1

August 2

August 3

August 4

August 5

August 6

August 7

August 8

August 9

August 10

August 11

August 12

August 13

August 14

August 15

August 16

August 17

August 18

August 19

August 20

_____

_____

August 21

_____

_____

_____

August 22

_____

_____

_____

August 23

_____

_____

_____

August 24

_____

_____

_____

August 25

_____

_____

_____

August 26

August 27

August 28

August 29

August 30

_____

_____

_____

August 31

_____

_____

_____

Flopsy, Mopsy, and Cotton-
tail who were good little
bunnies went down the lane to
gather blackberries.

SEPTEMBER

September 1

September 2

September 3

September 4

September 5

September 6

September 7

September 8

September 9

September 10

September 11

September 12

September 13

September 14

September 15

September 16

_____

_____

_____

September 17

_____

_____

_____

September 18

_____

_____

September 19

_____

_____

September 20

_____

_____

September 21

_____

_____

September 22

September 23

September 24

September 25

September 26

September 27

September 28

September 29

OCTOBER

October 1

October 2

October 3

October 4

October 5

October 6

October 7

October 8

_____

_____

October 9

_____

_____

October 10

_____

_____

October 11

_____

_____

October 12

October 13

October 14

October 15

October 16

October 17

October 18

October 19

October 20

_____

_____

_____

October 21

_____

_____

_____

October 22

October 23

October 24

October 25

October 26

October 27

October 28

October 29

October 30

October 31

NOVEMBER

November 1

November 2

November 3

November 4

November 5

November 6

November 7

November 8

_____

_____

_____

November 9

_____

_____

_____

November 10

_____

_____

_____

November 11

_____

_____

_____

November 12

November 13

November 14

November 15

November 16

November 17

November 18

_____

_____

_____

November 19

_____

_____

_____

November 20

_____

_____

_____

November 21

_____

_____

_____

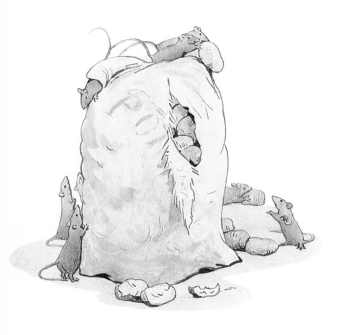

November 22

November 23

November 24

November 25

November 26

November 27

November 28

November 29

DECEMBER

December 1

_____

_____

December 2

_____

_____

December 3

_____

_____

_____

December 4

December 5

December 6

December 7

December 8

December 9

December 10

December 11

December 12

_____

_____

_____

December 13

_____

_____

_____

December 14

_____

_____

_____

December 15

_____

_____

_____

December 16

December 17

December 18

December 19

December 20

December 21

December 22

December 23

December 24

December 25

December 26

December 27

December 28

December 29

December 30

_____

_____

December 31

_____

_____

_____

SOURCES OF ILLUSTRATIONS